CHILDREN'S AUTHORS

JULIA ALVAREZ

Jill C. Wheeler

ABDO Publishing Company

visit us at
www.abdopublishing.com

Published by ABDO Publishing Company, 8000 West 78th Street, Edina, Minnesota 55439.
Copyright © 2012 by Abdo Consulting Group, Inc. International copyrights reserved in all
countries. No part of this book may be reproduced in any form without written permission from the
publisher. The Checkerboard Library™ is a trademark and logo of ABDO Publishing Company.

Printed in the United States of America, North Mankato, Minnesota.
062011
092011

 PRINTED ON RECYCLED PAPER

Cover Photo: AP Images
Interior Photos: Alamy p. 10; AP Images pp. 17, 21; Corbis p. 19; Getty Images p. 15;
    Thinkstock p. 13
    Photo copyright © Bill Eichner. By permission of Susan Bergholz Literary Services, New
    York, NY and Lamy, NM. All rights reserved. p. 5
    Photo courtesy of Julia Alvarez. By permission of Susan Bergholz Literary Services, New
    York, NY and Lamy, NM. All rights reserved. pp. 7, 8, 11

Series Coordinator: Megan M. Gunderson
Editors: BreAnn Rumsch, Megan M. Gunderson
Art Direction: Neil Klinepier

Library of Congress Cataloging-in-Publication Data

Wheeler, Jill C., 1964-
 Julia Alvarez / Jill C. Wheeler.
    p. cm. -- (Children's authors)
 Includes index.
 ISBN 978-1-61783-045-7
 1. Alvarez, Julia--Juvenile literature. 2. Authors, American--21st century--Biography--Juvenile
literature. 3. Hispanic American women authors--Biography--Juvenile literature. I. Title.
 PS3551.L845Z96 2011
 818'.5409--dc22
 [B]
                                        2011009739

CONTENTS

The Voice of Experience

Author Julia Alvarez believes the most exciting things happen in the places where two worlds blend together. That certainly has been true in her life. Alvarez has called both the Dominican Republic and the United States home. She spoke Spanish before she mastered English.

Alvarez has addressed this "between-ness" through her award-winning work. Her books explore what it is like to be adopted or to be an **immigrant**. They show how it feels when your homeland is in conflict. They help explain how it feels to be different from those around you.

Alvarez's work blends everything from personal experience to ancient legends and modern news headlines. Much of her writing features characters with roots in the Dominican Republic. Yet, their stories are familiar to anyone who has been caught between two worlds.

Getting teased as a child taught Alvarez the power of words.

ALL-AMERICAN

Julia Altagracia Alvarez was born on March 27, 1950, in New York City, New York. She was the second of four daughters born to Eduardo Alvarez and Julia Tavares de Alvarez. Eduardo was a doctor. He and his wife Julia were both from the Dominican Republic. But, they had met in the United States.

When Julia was just three months old, her family returned to the Dominican Republic. At the time, a **dictator** named Rafael Leónidas Trujillo Molina ruled the country. Trujillo's rule was marked by human rights abuses. It was dangerous for people to speak out against him.

Julia's family settled near her mother's relatives in Santo Domingo, the capital city. In those days, it was called Ciudad Trujillo in honor of the country's leader. There, Julia grew up surrounded by cousins, aunts, uncles, and maids. Her extended family lived in neighboring homes. Every summer, the family left the city to live by the beach.

Even while in the Dominican Republic, the Alvarez family was in love with America. They attended an American school called the Carol Morgan School. School was hard for Julia. But, she had a talent for memorizing poems after hearing them just a few times.

Julia (top right) with her parents and sisters, just before they left the Dominican Republic

ESCAPE TO NEW YORK

Julia's passport photo

The Tavares family was wealthy and influential. Julia's grandfather worked with the **United Nations**. So, her grandparents often went to the United States. Yet under Trujillo's rule, it was very hard for ordinary citizens to leave the Dominican Republic. When Julia was 10, she learned her family would travel to the United States. Julia was thrilled!

When she arrived, Julia learned that her family had not left for a visit. They had fled to New York to escape Trujillo and save their lives. Julia later learned that her father had been involved in a plot to remove Trujillo from power. Trujillo had planned to arrest Eduardo. But the family had escaped just in time.

Julia was excited to be in New York. But life in America was not always easy. Some classmates laughed at her imperfect English. Julia felt lonely. She missed her friends and family back on the island. But in time, her homesickness passed.

Julia's grades also improved. At first, she attended a Catholic elementary school. Then at age 13, Julia became a student at Abbot Academy in Andover, Massachusetts. Her mother had attended the school, and her sisters would, too.

As a teenager, Julia spent summers back in the Dominican Republic. There, she chose to speak English even with family. She was growing more distant from her island past.

FINDING A PASSION FOR WORDS

Middlebury College

In high school, Julia realized she wanted to be a writer. Her Dominican **culture** and family did not encourage women to have careers. Yet a writing assignment in English class made Julia think of a different path for herself. Writing about her life helped Julia understand why she felt so alone and different.

Julia graduated from high school in 1967. Then, she began attending Connecticut College in New London. Julia thrived at college. She won the school's Benjamin T. Marshall Poetry Prize in both 1968 and 1969. The award honors the best original poem.

Julia (right) on her first day of college in 1967

During summer 1969, Julia attended the Bread Loaf Writers' Conference. It is held each year at Middlebury College's Bread Loaf campus in Ripton, Vermont. Julia quickly decided she must transfer to Middlebury. There, she became more firmly convinced she wanted to be a writer. Julia graduated with **honors** in 1971.

Julia briefly worked at a newsletter before deciding to attend graduate school. She earned a masters degree in creative writing from Syracuse University in New York in 1975. While there, Julia won the Academy of American Poetry Prize.

Migrant Poet

After graduation, Alvarez hit the road! She piled everything she owned into a yellow Volkswagen Beetle. Alvarez drove to Kentucky, where she worked for the Kentucky Arts Commission. For two years, she helped schoolchildren and community members with their writing.

After that, Alvarez taught in California. Then in winter 1978, she worked on a **bilingual** writing project in Delaware. In spring 1978, Alvarez went to North Carolina to lead poetry workshops.

People were not always sure why Alvarez was there. One time, a man showed up to talk about poultry, not poetry! Alvarez discovered the man had never learned to read or write. But, he recited a poem he had made up. Alvarez wrote it down for him.

From 1979 to 1981, Alvarez taught English and creative writing at Phillips Academy in Andover. The boarding school she had attended was now part of this school.

Next, Alvarez taught at the University of Vermont in Burlington, George Washington University in Washington, D.C., and the University of Illinois in Urbana. In winter 1988, she lived as a resident writer at an artists' colony in the Dominican Republic.

Alvarez enjoyed seeing different places and sharing her love of words with new people. In one 15-year period, she had 18 different addresses! She called herself a **migrant** poet.

The Dominican Republic is an island nation in the Caribbean Sea. It shares the island of Hispaniola with the country of Haiti.

ROOTS & BOOKS

Alvarez's life provided rich material for a writer. She published poems and essays in small magazines. Then in 1984, she published her first book of poetry. It is called *Homecoming*. Many of the poems describe things that really happened to Alvarez.

In 1988, Alvarez returned to Middlebury to teach English. The next year, she married Bill Eichner. She had been married two other times, but neither marriage had worked out. Her new husband was an **ophthalmologist** who had grown up on a farm in Nebraska. His and Alvarez's lives could hardly have seemed more different!

Meanwhile, Alvarez had been working on short stories. A **literary agent** helped her submit them together as one book. They became her first published novel, *How the García Girls Lost Their Accents*. The book came out in 1991. Critics and readers loved it.

The story of the Mirabal sisters is still remembered in the Dominican Republic.

In 1994, Alvarez's second novel was published. *In the Time of the Butterflies* tells the true story of the four Mirabal sisters in the Dominican Republic. Like Alvarez's father, they work to remove Trujillo from power. The book became a movie in 2001. It inspired a dance production called *Las Mariposas*, or "The Butterflies," more than 15 years after its publication.

Inspired to Try Something New

Throughout the 1990s, Alvarez continued to publish her writing and win awards. She wrote *¡Yo!*, a novel that returned to characters from the *García Girls*. She also wrote two books of poetry and a book of essays called *Something to Declare*.

In 1996, Alvarez and her husband purchased a small farm in the Dominican Republic. Today, the farm covers about 260 acres (105 ha) of land. It combines a **sustainable** coffee-growing operation with a small school.

Alvarez and Eichner wanted to teach basic reading and writing skills to local residents at their school. There, Alvarez began using picture books to help teach her students. This inspired her to publish her first children's book in 2000.

Alvarez based her picture book *The Secret Footprints* on a legend she heard growing up in the Dominican Republic. It is about a group of women who live underwater and only come out at night. No one has ever seen them because they hold a special secret. Alvarez remembers lying awake at night hoping to spot one of these special women.

Alvarez and Eichner named their farm **Alta Gracia,** *which means "high grace."*

17

Introducing Tía Lola

Alvarez continued writing for young readers with her next book. She had grown up surrounded by aunts, or *tías*. Alvarez had missed them when her family had moved to New York.

So, Alvarez rolled all of her aunts and their **unique** personalities into one character. That character is Tía Lola. She first appeared in *How Tía Lola Came to ~~Visit~~ Stay* in 2001. Young readers loved the story of a Dominican version of Mary Poppins.

Alvarez followed the funny Tía Lola book with a more serious novel for young adults. She published *Before We Were Free* in 2002. It is about a young Dominican girl who lives in fear of a cruel **dictator**. Alvarez based it on her extended family's experiences. The book won the 2003 **Pura Belpré Award**.

Alvarez won the Pura Belpré Award again in 2010 for *Return to Sender*. This young readers novel was also added to Oprah Winfrey's 2010 Kids' Reading List. The story illustrates the experiences of many modern children of **migrant** workers. It also addresses the challenges children face when their parents are in the United States illegally.

Success did not come early for Alvarez. She was 41 and had been writing for more than 20 years when her first novel was finally published.

At Peace in Two Worlds

Today, Alvarez and her husband divide their time between Vermont and their farm in the Dominican Republic. The farm has already shown up in Alvarez's writing. Published in 2001, *A Cafecito Story* features several people who learned to read and write at her school.

Alvarez also wrote a book about the **patron saint** after which her farm is named. *A Gift of Gracias: The Legend of Altagracia* was published in 2005. It tells the story of the Virgin of Altagracia, after whom Alvarez is also named. The book was published in English and Spanish at the same time.

Alvarez has since returned to Tía Lola. *How Tía Lola Learned to Teach* was released in October 2010. Alvarez planned two more additions to the popular series for 2011. They were *How Tía Lola Saved the Summer* and *How Tía Lola Ended Up Starting Over*. Alvarez loves to challenge herself with her work. So, readers look forward to whatever she will write next!

In 2010, Alvarez promoted her new Tía Lola book with a blog tour.

GLOSSARY

bilingual - having or being written in two different languages.

culture - the customs, arts, and tools of a nation or a people at a certain time.

dictator - a ruler with complete control who often governs in a cruel way.

honors - special attention given to a graduating student for high academic achievement.

immigrant - a person who enters another country to live.

literary agent - a person who helps an author sell his or her work.

migrant - a person who moves regularly in order to find work.

ophthalmologist (ahf-thuhl-MAH-luh-jihst) - a doctor who deals with the structure, functions, and diseases of the eye.

patron saint - a saint believed to be the special protector of a church, a city, a state, or a country.

Pura Belpré Award - an annual award given by the American Library Association. It honors writers and illustrators whose work for children celebrates the Latino cultural experience.

sustainable - relating to a method of using a resource so that the resource is not used up or damaged.

unique - being the only one of its kind.

United Nations - a group of nations formed in 1945. Its goals are peace, human rights, security, and social and economic development.

WEB SITES

To learn more about Julia Alvarez, visit ABDO Publishing Company online. Web sites about Julia Alvarez are featured on our Book Links page. These links are routinely monitored and updated to provide the most current information available.

www.abdopublishing.com

INDEX